Katie Taylor

50

fantastic ideas for mud kitchens

BLOOMSBURY

BLOOMSBURY EDUCATION
Bloomsbury Publishing Plc
50 Bedford Square, London WC1B 3DP, UK
Bloomsbury Publishing Ireland Limited
29 Earlsfort Terrace, Dublin 2, D02 AY28, Ireland

BLOOMSBURY, BLOOMSBURY EDUCATION and the Diana logo are trademarks
of Bloomsbury Publishing Plc

First published in Great Britain, 2026 by Bloomsbury Publishing Plc
This edition published in Great Britain, 2026 by Bloomsbury Publishing Plc

A catalogue record for this book is available from the British Library

ISBN: PB: 978-1-80199-796-6

2 4 6 8 10 9 7 5 3 1 (paperback)

Design concept by Lynda Murray
Text design by Laura Neate

Printed and bound in India by Replika Press Pvt. Ltd

To find out more about our authors and books visit www.bloomsbury.com and sign up for our newsletters.
For product safety related questions contact productsafety@bloomsbury.com

*I would like to say a huge thank you to all of my family and friends, especially the young children for helping
to test out my ideas and be models for the mud kitchen book. Also, a special thank you to Precision Timber
who donated their wonderful mud kitchen.*

Contents

Introduction

A mud kitchen is a popular item for educators and parents to include in an outdoor space designed for young children. In years gone by, children have always enjoyed creating mud pies by mixing up mud in the garden. Some of my own fondest memories of early childhood involve making creations in the dirt. The mud kitchen has evolved over time and is now an exciting place to mix, concoct, explore and experiment in.

A mud kitchen space does not need to be fancy or elaborate and can take as much space up as you wish to provide. There is a mud kitchen for every budget as you can make your own or purchase one already made. Borrow from nature for the ingredients and let Mother Earth guide you through the seasons when setting up a mud kitchen. Items to include in the mud kitchen can be bought new, found in charity shops, donated by friends or relatives or purchased from internet selling sites. The saying 'one man's trash is another man's treasure' relates well when thinking of mud kitchen accessories to include.

Building your own mud kitchen can be a fun, collaborative project for all to become involved in. An old sink, bowls or tubs are perfect for mixing mud, sand and water in. Include a variety of utensils such as spoons, sieves, ladles, spatulas and graters. It is also a good idea to offer a workspace for children to work on where they can spread out and be as creative as they wish.

Autumn can be a great time to stock up on nature's treasure. When exploring in the outdoors, forage for fallen items from nature such as pinecones, sticks, pebbles, leaves and petals to use as ingredients. Always remember to leave plenty for wildlife and only borrow if there is an abundance. Display in bowls, jars or bottles for children to access independently.

A natural space near the mud kitchen that offers a space to grow and dig for mud will be beneficial to the children. Herbs that are easy to grow or wildflowers that return year after year not only benefit wildlife, but once they have wilted can serve as an ingredient to the mud kitchen. Look in supermarkets at the end of the day for reduced bunches of flowers or ask friends and relatives for their used bunches. When looking to fill the mud kitchen with mud, it is best to avoid compost as this does not mould the same as mud will. If buying, look for a good quality topsoil or use freshly dug molehills.

This book aims to encourage children (and adults) to be creative in the mud kitchen and shows parents, carers and Early Years practitioners how to use the mud kitchen to help the children make progress in all seven areas of learning in the Early Years Foundation Stage (EYFS). It is not designed to be a prescriptive 'must follow' set of instructions but to guide and inspire. The children can build upon the activities included and adapt them according to their own wonderful ideas. As adults, we can provide the materials, ingredients and utensils to encourage the children's play and allow them to explore and create as they wish. Step back and observe the children's play and become involved if the children invite you to. Offer items to extend their skills such as tweezers to pick up the items from nature or smaller utensils to build up fine motor skills once ready.

It's time to roll up your sleeves, get your hands dirty and cook up some muddy creations!

How to use this book

The pages are all organised in the same way. Before you start any activity, read through everything on the page so that you are familiar with the whole activity and what you might need to plan in advance.

What you need lists the resources required for the activity. These are likely to be readily available in most settings or can be bought or made easily.

What to do tells you step-by-step what you need to do to complete the activity.

Top tips are helpful hints to make an activity work well and have been learned from experience!

The **Health & Safety** tips are often obvious, but safety cannot be overstressed. In many cases, there are no specific hazards involved in completing the activity, and your usual health and safety measure should be enough. In others, there are particular issues to be noted and addressed.

Taking it forward gives ideas for additional activities on the same theme, or for developing the activity further. These will be particularly useful for things that have gone especially well or where children show a real interest. In many cases they use the same resources, and in every case they have been designed to extend learning and broaden the children's experiences.

What's in it for the children? tells you (and others) briefly how the suggested activities contribute to learning. Where any of the EYFS seven areas of learning (communication and language, personal, emotional and social development, physical development, literacy, mathematics, understanding of the world and expressive art and design) have been linked to, they will be highlighted in **bold**.

Make your own mud kitchen

What you need:

- Two log stumps
- A wooden plank
- Mud
- Pots, pans and bowls
- Kitchen utensils (optional)

What's in it for the children?

Working together to create their own recipes in a homemade mud kitchen encourages **problem solving** and **collaboration** with others. This type of mud kitchen is just as much fun as a pre-made one.

Taking it forward

- Add extra items such as a sink or drinks dispenser to enhance the play.

What to do:

1. Place the two logs stumps onto a flat part of the ground.
2. Lay the plank across the top. This will be the worktop of the mud kitchen.
3. Place the pots and pans onto the plank and the ground around it.
4. Use the space under the plank for the oven.
5. Get the children busy mixing up muddy recipes in the new mud kitchen!

Health & Safety

Make sure that the plank is steady on the logs to ensure it doesn't fall over onto the children when playing.

Top tip

If there are no logs available, use two crates to balance the plank on instead.

Open ended mud kitchen

What you need:

- A water source
- Mud, sand and water
- Containers: bowls, tins, moulds, dishes, cups, mugs, jars, jugs and bottles
- Utensils: spoons, ladles, sieves, tongs, safety scissors and mashers
- Items from nature: pinecones, pebbles, feathers, seeds, leaves, petals, flowers, grasses, plants, sticks or logs

What's in it for the children?

Exposure to outdoor, free play is beneficial to children in many ways. It can also give children a sense of wellbeing. Open ended mud kitchen play promotes resilience, helping children learn how to **communicate** and **problem solve** while **creating** and **exploring**.

Taking it forward

- Follow the children's lead and observe how and what they play with.
- Extend this by offering more challenging resources and utensils, for example a garlic press or small grater.

Top tip 

Build up the mud kitchen resources over time by asking the children's parents or your own relatives and friends to donate items they no longer need, or visit car boot sales and charity shops.

What to do:

1. An open ended mud kitchen is filled with possibilities for the children. Arrange the items at child level and ensure they are easily accessible.

2. Provide a variety of natural materials as well as a good amount of mud.

3. Set up a water source such as a drinks dispenser, bucket filled with water or an attached sink. This allows children to work with water freely.

4. Play alongside the children or stand back and observe them playing independently.

5. Leave creations and recipes out for children to return to at a later date, allowing them to extend and build on their previous play.

Health & Safety

Always check mud kitchen items before the next use to ensure that none are broken, rusty or sharp.

Sand kitchen
Swap mud for sand

What you need:

- Different coloured play sand
- Water
- Containers: bowls, jugs, cups
- Utensils: spoons, scoops, mashers
- A measuring jug (optional)
- Items from nature

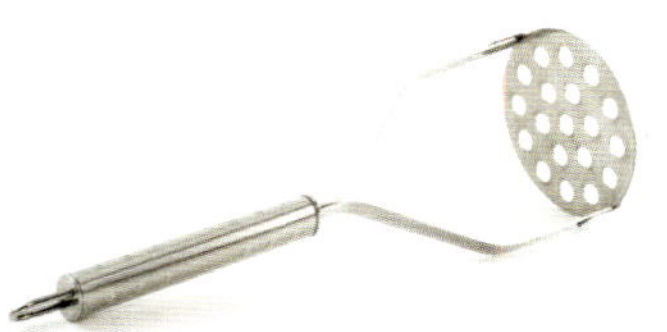

What to do:

1. Provide different colours or kinds of sand, such as kinetic sand.

2. Fill a variety of different bowls and containers with sand and have a jug of water ready.

3. Encourage the children to play with the sand and explore the different consistencies when water is added. Discuss concepts of measurement with older children, encouraging them to measure out different amounts of water and see what effects these have on the sand.

4. Encourage the children to use the sand to 'bake' with, create recipes and mix up new concoctions.

5. Include items found in nature as additional ingredients to encourage children to experiment with cooking and decorating.

What's in it for the children?

Sand is a very tactile medium; manipulating and exploring the texture of sand helps the children to enhance their **fine motor skills** and **hand-eye coordination**. Introducing the idea of measurement to older children will help to develop their **mathematical understanding**.

Taking it forward

- Continue the sand play in a sandpit or sand tray. Observe how the children connect with the sand in the mud kitchen and provide similar utensils and opportunities in the sandpit on a larger scale.

✚ Health & Safety

Only use play sand and not builders' sand as this is not suitable for children. Change play sand regularly and mix and turn it to ensure that it stays aerated.

Top tip ⭐

Slowly adding water to the sand changes the consistency so that it can be moulded with hands. This can be used to create cakes, cupcakes or any other sand recipes you can think of!

Autumn mud kitchen

Nature's loose parts in the mud kitchen

What you need:

- Autumn leaves (variety of colours)
- Autumn nature finds: sticks, acorns, conkers, pinecones, alder cones
- Vocabulary labels (optional)
- Bowls
- Mud

What's in it for the children?

This activity helps to develop the children's **understanding of the world** and seasonal changes, as well as encouraging **communication** and **literacy** skills through introducing new vocabulary. Making their own creations will develop their **expressive art and design** skills and give them a sense of pride in their work.

Taking it forward

- Head outdoors to spot the beauty of autumn all around. Can the children discover their own nature finds and identify which tree they came from?
- Explore the new vocabulary of the different tree names and seeds and nuts found in autumn.

Health & Safety

Check the allergies of the children and adults in the setting and complete a risk assessment when using small nature finds.

What to do:

1. Discuss with the children about what they already know about autumn, or what changes or weather they might see in autumn.

2. Add a variety of different coloured foraged leaves to the mud kitchen, including reds, browns, golden colours and yellows.

3. Add autumnal items from nature – store them in containers, bowls or tubs. Add vocabulary labels about autumn as an extra visual prompt.

4. Fill the bowls with mud.

5. Encourage the children to mix, create and explore using the leaves, mud and autumnal items. Use descriptive vocabulary (such as golden, crisp, crimson, crunchy and so on) and help the children to explore sensory aspects such as textures, sounds and colours.

6. Invite the children to make up their own autumn-inspired recipes.

Top tip 

When foraging for autumn nature finds, make sure not to take too much from one area and leave plenty for wildlife.

Halloween kitchen

What you need:

- Books or stories about Halloween (optional)
- Pumpkins or squash (varying shapes and sizes)
- Halloween decorations
- Slime or coloured water
- Utensils
- Cauldrons

Top tip 

Be mindful that some children may be sensitive to the spooky or scary elements of Halloween before decorating your mud kitchen and tone it down if needed.

What's in it for the children?

This activity helps the children to have an exciting sensory experience using slime or coloured water as an alternative to mud. They will use **communication and language** skills while marvelling at their concoctions and develop **literacy** skills when making up spells or stories.

Taking it forward

- Grow your own pumpkins for use in the mud kitchen. Sow seeds indoors in April and plant outdoors (in a sunny, sheltered spot) at the end of May to the beginning of June once the last frost has passed.

- Save the seeds from inside the pumpkins for an added ingredient in the mud kitchen.

What to do:

1. Discuss with the children what they know about Halloween, magic or witches and link it to stories that they may have read such as *Room on the Broom* by Julia Donaldson.

2. Decorate the mud kitchen with Halloween decorations such as cobwebs, signs, pumpkins, cauldrons or spiders.

3. Fill bowls with slime or coloured water and add a range of utensils.

4. Discover with the children what happens when mixing, stirring and concocting with slime or coloured water. Encourage the children to discuss what they are doing while they are exploring.

5. Foster the children's creativity by suggesting that they make a witch's brew using the ingredients, thinking of a magic spell or making up their own Halloween stories.

Potion station
Turn the mud kitchen magical

What you need:

- An assortment of different sized bottles
- Cauldrons or bowls
- Measuring jug (optional)
- Mud
- Water
- Items from nature
- Utensils
- Sticks

Top tip 

Create magic wands from sticks to enhance magical play and use within potion making..

What's in it for the children?

Creating recipe instructions together helps the children develop their **listening** skills and pouring liquids helps the children with mealtime confidence and the pouring of their own drinks. Exploring the measuring, mixing and creating of potions helps the children to develop an early **mathematical** understanding of capacity.

Taking it forward

- Try out chemical reactions in mud kitchen bowls using bicarbonate of soda, white vinegar and washing up liquid. The potions will fizz and crackle as the children experiment with different amounts of ingredients.

- Link the activity to well-known picture books featuring wizards, witches, potions and spells as part of the children's literacy learning.

What to do:

1. Fill the mud kitchen with a range of bottles, cauldrons, bowls, utensils, sticks, items from nature, water and mud.

2. Discuss with the children which potions they might make and how they might make them. Talk to older children about measurement and how to use a measuring jug.

3. Encourage the children to experiment with making their own potions by adding ingredients into the cauldrons or bowls and stirring them. Encourage the children to make up their own spells and share them with each other.

4. Gather the children and collect their ideas for a potion recipe. Write it out for others to follow or to put on display in the setting.

Health & Safety

If choosing to use glass bottles, risk assess and observe at all times in case of breakages. Alternatively, use recycled plastic or metal.

Diwali mud kitchen

Celebrate the festival of lights

What you need:

- Books about Diwali or pictures of Diwali celebrations (optional)
- Diwali decorations such as diya lamps (optional)
- Mud
- Bowls
- Utensils: safety scissors, tongs, jugs
- Items from nature: petals, leaves, pebbles

What's in it for the children?

The children will enhance their **understanding of the world** by learning about and celebrating other cultures. Introducing new vocabulary and stories helps to develop their **communication and literacy** skills and using leaves to make Rangoli patterns helps to improve their **fine motor skills**.

Taking it forward

- Create long lasting Rangoli patterns on pebbles or log slices to include in the children's play.

What to do:

1. Discuss with the children what they might already know about Diwali: when, how and why it is celebrated.

2. Introduce the children to new vocabulary (such as Rangoli, Diya, Mehndi, Rama, Sita and so on). Read the story of Rama and Sita with the children, show them what a Rangoli pattern looks like and discuss different foods eaten on Diwali such as Barfi (a sweet fudge containing spices or nuts) and Samosas (triangular shaped pastries that include spices).

3. Create a mud kitchen set up that includes plenty of mud and items from nature. A reduced, donated or wilted bunch of flowers or cuttings from your own garden would be the perfect addition to the Diwali mud kitchen.

4. Include utensils, safety scissors and tongs to encourage the children to use a range of resources, in turn enhancing their fine motor skills.

5. Show the children how to make Rangoli patterns in the mud kitchen bowls or encourage them to mix up a traditional dish served during the celebration.

6. Encourage the children's pride in their work by taking pictures of their creations to include in a colourful Diwali display.

Health & Safety

If choosing to use diya lamps with an artificial tealight, ensure the battery component cannot be accessed by children as they are extremely harmful if swallowed.

Acorn mud pie

An autumn delight

What you need:

- Mud and water
- A dish or tin
- Acorns

What's in it for the children?

This activity helps children to gain an **understanding of the life cycle of a tree**, while fostering their creativity through **imaginative play**. Arranging the acorns into patterns helps foster both **mathematical understanding** of pattern and shape and **expressive art and design** skills.

Taking it forward

- Teach the children about acorns and their growth into trees over time.

- Plant an acorn in a jar to see the roots growing and once established, plant outdoors and see if an oak tree grows.

Health & Safety

Ensure young children do not place acorns in their mouths as this could become a choking hazard. Risk assess and swap acorns for something different for children under three.

What to do:

1. Talk to the children about what they know about acorns, where they come from and how they grow. Explain that the children are going to use acorns to make a pie.

2. Show the children how to stir the water into mud to create a sloppy consistency and let them experiment.

3. Help the children to scoop the muddy mixture into a tin, filling it to the top.

4. Ask the children to decorate the top of the pie with acorns and other found items from nature. Discuss with the children how to make a pattern and encourage them to make their own.

5. Encourage imaginative play by asking the children to 'bake' their pies in the mud kitchen oven and 'serve' with stick chips and muddy gravy.

Top tip ⭐

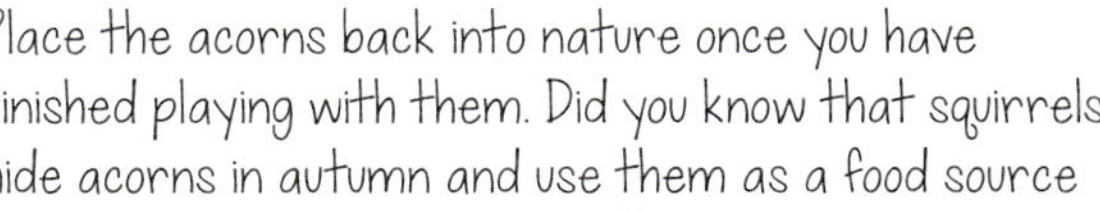

Place the acorns back into nature once you have finished playing with them. Did you know that squirrels hide acorns in autumn and use them as a food source in winter when there is no food?

Pinecone mud crumble

What you need:

- *The Gruffalo* book (optional)
- Water
- Dry mud
- Pinecones
- Tins
- Spoons

What to do:

1. Read *The Gruffalo* with the children and discuss how they could make their own 'Gruffalo crumbles' by using mud and pinecones.

2. Stir a small amount of water into the dry mud mixture and add a few pinecones.

3. Show the children how to fill the tins with the mixture, leaving a little space at the top for the crumble.

4. Encourage the children to sprinkle dry mud onto the top, creating a crumble effect, and decorate with a layer of pinecones.

5. Suggest that the children 'bake' the crumble in the mud kitchen oven and role play 'serving' with muddy ice-cream.

✚ Health & Safety

Remove bugs from pinecones by soaking in a bucket of warm water and a cup of white vinegar for around an hour. Leave to dry.

What's in it for the children?

Mixing and stirring the muddy mixture and handling the mud kitchen tools helps to develop the children's **strength**, **coordination** and **gross motor skills**. Linking their mud kitchen play to stories that they have read helps to develop their **literacy** skills.

Taking it forward

- Try a pinecone experiment with the children: place an open pinecone into water and see how it closes up to protect the seeds. Leave somewhere warm and dry to observe how it opens back up again. This is to help release the seeds inside into the world for new trees to grow.

Top tip 

Collect fallen pinecones from pine trees, but leave plenty for wildlife. September to December is the best time to collect as they usually fall in autumn.

Muddy drinks kitchen

An imaginative play café

What you need:

- Mud
- Water
- Cups or mugs
- Jugs or a water dispenser
- Spoons
- Sticks
- Squirty foam (optional)
- Items from nature (optional)
- Old teabags (optional)

What to do:

1. Explain to the children that today they can be baristas in their very own muddy café!

2. Fill jugs with water or a water dispenser to ensure the children have access to plenty of water in their play.

3. Include dry mud, sticks, items from nature, squirty foam and spoons in the mud kitchen.

4. Show the children how to make muddy coffees by putting a spoonful of dry mud into a cup or mug and pouring water in.

5. Encourage the children to stir their mixture with a stick or spoon until it gets to the right consistency. They can also add squirty foam on top for a frothy coffee.

6. Use old teabags with muddy water for a 'refreshing' cup of tea.

7. Sprinkle items from nature on top for added decoration.

8. Encourage the children to have fun mixing, stirring, pouring and creating a variety of drinks.

Top tip ⭐

Recycle takeaway cups or search charity shops for old or metal mugs and save used teabags to incorporate into the play.

What's in it for the children?

Pouring, emptying and filling helps the children gain a **mathematical understanding** of capacity through their own exploration. Role playing a café setting helps the children develop their **imaginative play** and **communication** skills.

Taking it forward

- Try making new flavours by adding in different ingredients. For example, sand for a caramel flavoured drink or herbs such as mint for a muddy minty hot chocolate.

➕ Health & Safety

Reiterate that the drinks are pretend and not for drinking. Model pretend air sipping to the children.

Winter mud kitchen

Wrap up warm and head outdoors

What you need:

- Ice and snow
- Green winter foliage
- Pinecones
- Winter vocabulary (optional)
- Scoops
- Bowls
- Pans
- Utensils
- Log slices

What to do:

1. Make sure that the children are wrapped up warm.
2. Fill the mud kitchen bowls with ice and snow.
3. Decorate the mud kitchen with green winter foliage and include any winter items from nature available. Include winter vocabulary labels for older children.
4. Offer scoops, bowls, pans, utensils and log slices.
5. Encourage the children to explore the snow and ice, using the pans and utensils to mix new recipes and winter stews. Talk to the children while they are exploring: what new textures, colours and smells have they noticed?

Health & Safety

Wear gloves when handling ice to avoid hurting little fingers.

What's in it for the children?

Playing outdoors during the winter months teaches children that they do not have to wait for warm weather to enjoy some outdoor fun. During winter, any time spent outdoors is beneficial for the children's health and **physical development**.

Taking it forward

- Take the children's learning further by teaching them about snow and how it is formed in the atmosphere.
- Look at snowflakes and their patterns. Did you know that every snowflake is unique and you will never find two the same?

Top tip

Wrap up in layers, hats and gloves during colder months to enjoy outdoor play for longer. Use eco-friendly artificial snow if there is no real snow available.

Frozen snow cake

Make the most of seasonal changes

What you need:

- Snow
- Round bowls or tins
- Scoops
- Winter decorations
- Cranberries (optional)

If using cranberries with children under three, cut them into quarters lengthways to avoid a choking hazard.

What's in it for the children?

Learning about seasonal changes, melting and freezing all help to develop the children's **understanding of the world**. Working together on their cakes helps to foster a sense of teamwork and improve their **communication and language** skills.

Taking it forward

- Leave the snow cake out overnight and help the children to observe what happens. If the temperature drops below zero degrees, explore the consistency of the snow. Has it frozen? If the temperature is warm, does the snow melt?

What to do:

1. Explain to the children that they will be making a snow cake and collect their ideas about how they could make it and what they think it could look like.

2. Encourage the children to work together and follow your instructions to make a snow cake.

3. Show the children how to scoop snow into a bowl until it is full.

4. Help the children work together to turn the bowl over and lift away to reveal a cake shape.

5. Look for items in nature together or use cranberries and other winter decorations.

6. Encourage the children to decorate the cake with the items from nature around the edges and on top and serve on wooden log slices.

7. Extend the children's learning about melting and freezing by asking questions such as 'what would happen if we left it out overnight?' Discuss with the children other experiments that they could do with snow.

Christmas mud kitchen

Give the mud kitchen a festive makeover

What you need:

- Bowls
- Snow
- Mud
- Foliage
- Pots and pans
- Festive items: dried citrus, cranberries, cinnamon sticks, pinecones, carrots, sprouts
- Old Christmas mugs (optional)
- Squirty foam (optional)

What to do:

1. Talk to the children about what they already know about Christmas and any festive traditions they might do at home.

2. Fill the bowls with mud and snow. Decorate with evergreen foliage all around the mud kitchen.

3. Add festive items: dried citrus, cranberries, cinnamon sticks, pinecones, carrots or sprouts, old Christmas mugs and any decorations.

4. Encourage the children to have fun mixing and concocting festive recipes. Use the cranberries or cinnamon sticks to place on top of muddy Christmas drinks with a little squirty foam and garnish with items from nature.

5. Encourage the children to use the carrots, sprouts, cranberries or dried citrus to experiment with Christmas themed soups, lunches, dinner and recipe ideas.

Health & Safety

Explain that the items in the Christmas mud kitchen are for play and not for consumption. Always complete a risk assessment.

What's in it for the children?

Celebrating a festive tradition and encouraging the children to play through their own experiences of Christmas helps to develop their **communication and social skills** and **understanding of the world**. Experimenting with different textures in an outdoor setting gives the children a positive sensory experience.

Taking it forward

- Extend the children's learning by reading Christmas stories and singing Christmas songs. Create an entire Christmas dinner using the mud kitchen items and ingredients. Use bark for the meat, sticks and leaves for vegetables and watery mud for the gravy. Serve on log slices or plates from the mud kitchen.

Top tip 

Be mindful that not all the children celebrate Christmas and discuss with them the different traditions or festivals they might celebrate instead.

Gingerbread mud cookies

A classic winter recipe

What you need:

- Mud
- Water
- Flour
- Ground ginger, cinnamon or nutmeg (optional)
- Bowls
- Spoons
- Gingerbread cutters
- Baking trays
- Items from nature

What's in it for the children?

Mixing mud with their hands and feeling different textures as the mud turns from sloppy to a thicker consistency is an excellent sensory experience and connects the children with nature.

Rolling helps to build **gross motor skills** and strength in the arms, shoulders and core, whilst decorating the gingerbread men helps to develop **fine motor skills**.

Taking it forward

- Read the story *The Gingerbread Man* with the children to link the activity to literacy learning.
- Use a variety of different cutters to make different shapes.

What to do:

1. Scoop some mud into a bowl and mix in a little water. Sprinkle flour into the mud and stir. Keep adding a little more until the mud is a dough consistency, pouring a little water in if needed. Sprinkle in some ground ginger, cinnamon or nutmeg for an added sensory experience.

2. Show the children how to turn out the muddy dough and pat with hands so that it flattens. Alternatively, use a rolling pin (or a big stick) if one is available.

3. Help the children to press the gingerbread cutters into the muddy dough, removing the mud from the outside of the cutters.

4. Encourage the children to gently lay the muddy gingerbread characters into a baking tray and 'bake' in the mud kitchen oven.

5. Suggest that the children use items from nature to give the gingerbread mud cookies features, for example stones for their buttons and tiny leaves for eyes.

Health & Safety

Supervise the children carefully when using cutters and watch out for sharp edges, especially when pressing down.

Christmas puddings

A muddy twist on a traditional Christmas treat

What you need:

- Bowls
- Mud
- Water
- Squirty foam
- Cranberries
- Green foliage

What's in it for the children?

This activity helps the children to practise **bilateral skills** (the ability to use both hands in a coordinated way) by passing items from one hand to the other or steadying the bowl and mixing at the same time.

Taking it forward

- As an alternative, encourage the children to roll balls of mud in their hands to create a muddy mini-Christmas pudding. Top with squirty foam, berries and a touch of greenery.

Top tip ⭐

Use a green leaf that may be found during the winter months for the green foliage.

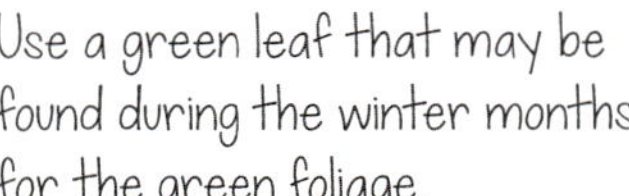

What to do:

1. Talk to the children about what Christmas puddings look like and show them pictures if they aren't sure.

2. Show the children how to mix up a thick, muddy mixture. Encourage them to get their hands in there and mix it together well.

3. Help the children to fill the bowls with plenty of the muddy mixture for the pudding.

4. Encourage the children to squirt the squirty foam onto the top third of the bowl and add the decorations of cranberries and green foliage.

➕ Health & Safety

Cranberries can pose a choking hazard to young children. If necessary, cut the cranberries lengthways in half to prevent this or use an alternative item. Most wild berries are poisonous and should be avoided in play.

Muddy hot chocolate

Unleash your creativity by making a muddy drink

What you need:

- Water
- Jugs
- Water dispenser (optional)
- Spoons or scoops
- Mud
- Cups and mugs
- Sticks
- Squirty foam

Top tip 

Squirty soap foam is an excellent children's alternative to shaving foam and is available to buy cheaply.

What's in it for the children?

Using the squirty foam is brilliant for building up **finger strength** and **fine motor skills** which are key for when children begin their writing journey. A child's hands will benefit from plenty of activities such as this along with squeezing, pressing and manipulating objects.

Taking it forward

- Explore filling and emptying other containers and discuss capacity.

What to do:

1. Pour water into jugs for the children to use, alternatively, use a water dispenser for the children to access freely.

2. Show the children how to scoop a spoonful of mud into a cup and fill with water.

3. Encourage the children to stir with a stick or spoon and add more mud until it looks like hot chocolate.

4. Show the children how to use the squirty foam on top of the muddy hot chocolate drink. Move around the top of the cup in a circular motion.

5. Encourage the children to sprinkle extra mud on top and place a stick in for a pretend chocolate treat.

Health & Safety

Check for skin allergies when using squirty foam.

Muddy noodles

Served fresh with mud

What you need:

- Mud
- Bowls
- Frying pan
- Safety scissors
- Wool or string
- Items from nature
- Sticks or chopsticks

Health & Safety

When discarding mud back into the earth after play, remove any non-natural materials before doing so.

What's in it for the children?

Following simple instructions helps to develop children's **listening skills** and understanding of new vocabulary. Using chopsticks helps to build **hand strength** and develop **fine motor skills**.

Taking it forward

- Encourage the children to use chopsticks to move the noodles from one bowl to another. Incorporate counting to add a mathematical element to the activity.

What to do:

1. In the mud kitchen bowls, stir and mix a muddy mixture together. This will be the soy sauce.

2. Show the children how to use safety scissors to cut different lengths of wool or string. Stir them into the muddy bowls.

3. Encourage the children to 'fry' some natural ingredients such as petals, flowers and leaves for the meat and vegetables.

4. Show the children how to stir them into the muddy noodle pan and 'cook' for a few more minutes.

5. Encourage the children to 'serve' the noodles to their friends and practise picking them up with chopsticks (or two sticks).

Top tip ⭐

Save chopsticks from takeaways and ask friends or relatives who enjoy knitting for any of their wool cut offs to use as muddy noodles.

Lunar New Year mud kitchen

Celebrating Lunar New Year

What you need:

- Lunar New Year decorations
- Bowls
- Mud
- Wool
- Red food colouring
- Water
- Chopsticks
- Items from nature

What to do:

1. Talk to the children about what they already know about Lunar New Year and how it is celebrated. Read a traditional Lunar New Year story with the children and discuss what they have understood from it.

2. Fill bowls with mud and decorate the mud kitchen with Lunar New Year decorations.

3. Mix red food colouring with water and include it in jugs and bowls.

4. Chop wool into pieces and display in bowls or containers. The wool can be used to create noodles in the mud.

5. Show the children how to use the chopsticks to pick up the muddy creations and ask the children to think of their own dishes to make.

6. Try creating some traditional dishes eaten at Lunar New Year such as chun juan (spring rolls), nian gao (sticky rice cake), dumplings or changshou mian (longevity noodles).

Top tip ⭐

Make chopsticks using two sticks by peeling the bark from the stick using a vegetable peeler and decorating using paint or pens.

Health & Safety
If making chopsticks using a peeler, wear a glove on the opposite hand and peel away from the body.

What's in it for the children?

Celebrating different cultures helps the children's **understanding of the world** and fosters inclusivity. Sharing traditional stories with them helps to develop their **listening skills** and talking about their mud kitchen creations helps to enhance their **communication and social skills**.

Taking it forward

- Learn more about Lunar New Year and the traditions that occur around the world when celebrating.

- Leave the items out all year to ensure cultures are reflected in the provision enhancements.

Mud and sand chocolates

A box full of delicious muddy chocolates

What you need:

- Recycled chocolate packaging
- Bowls and spoons
- Mud
- Water
- Sand
- Items from nature

What to do:

1. In bowls, mix up mud or sand, adding a little water if necessary.

2. Using the recycled chocolate packaging, show the children how to spoon mud or sand into the compartments to fill each one.

3. Encourage the children to decorate the muddy and sandy chocolates with a natural garnish.

4. Discuss with the children names that the chocolates could have such as 'leafy delight', 'muddy surprise' or 'sandy caramel'.

5. Let the children pretend to eat the chocolates and enjoy with a cup of muddy tea!

What's in it for the children?

Encouraging the children to use their imaginations to think of chocolate flavour ideas helps to develop their **communication and language skills**. Decorating the chocolates helps to develop fine motor and **expressive art and design** skills.

Taking it forward

- Design packaging for the chocolates created in the mud kitchen. Talk about when people might give each other chocolates and link to learning about Valentine's Day.

- Change the mud and sand for other sensory ingredients including squirty foam, playdough, bark chippings, leaves, stones or pebbles to make chocolates in the packaging.

Top tip ⭐

Once you have finished with the packaging, give it a rinse and pop it in the recycling.

Sandy pancakes
Life is better with pancakes

What you need:

- Sand
- Water
- Bowls
- Whisks
- Frying pans
- Spatulas
- Items from nature
- Lemons or citrus fruit (optional)

Top tip 

Add a little water and compact the sand tightly together for more successful flipping.

What's in it for the children?

Pivotal joints and **gross motor skills** are developed in children when the wrist, hands and arms are moved when flipping and frying the sandy pancakes. This is a perfect activity to build up these types of movements in in young children's bodies.

Taking it forward

- Continue the flipping motion activity using a range of objects in the frying pan to develop and build up the muscles in the upper body, arms and wrists.
- Add counting into the mix to develop the children's mathematical thinking. How many flips can they do?

What to do:

1. Discuss with the children about when they might eat pancakes, for example on Pancake Day.

2. In a bowl, whisk sand and a splash of water together to make a pancake batter.

3. Show the children how to pour the mixture into the frying pan and 'cook' on the mud kitchen hob for a few minutes.

4. Help the children to try flipping the sandy pancakes with a spatula.

5. Encourage the children to add their favourite toppings such as petal strawberries, sliced citrus fruits, pinecones or flowers.

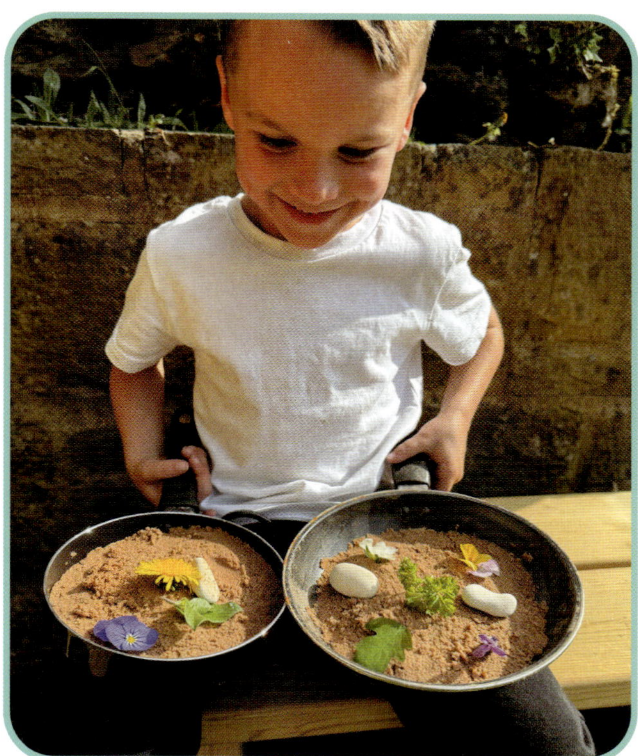

Health & Safety

When flipping the pancakes, aim away from the face to ensure sand does not land in the eyes. If this happens, blink and rinse with clean water very gently.

Spring mud kitchen

New life and spring colours

What you need:

- Mud
- Coloured water
- Bowls or tubs
- Spring flowers, petals or blossoms
- Green leaves
- Plants
- Utensils
- Safety scissors

What to do:

1. Discuss with the children what they already know about spring and what changes they have noticed outside.

2. Fill bowls or tubs with mud and include a range of utensils.

3. Create coloured water and add petals to it. Place in bowls or jars.

4. Provide a range of spring plants, flowers and leaves for the children to use in their muddy creations. The children can cut, snip, tear and mash the petals or leaves into their recipes.

5. Support the children to use their senses when exploring the spring mud kitchen. What does it smell like? What does it feel like in their hands?

6. Encourage the children to create their own spring recipes such as petal pie, blossom soup and flower buns.

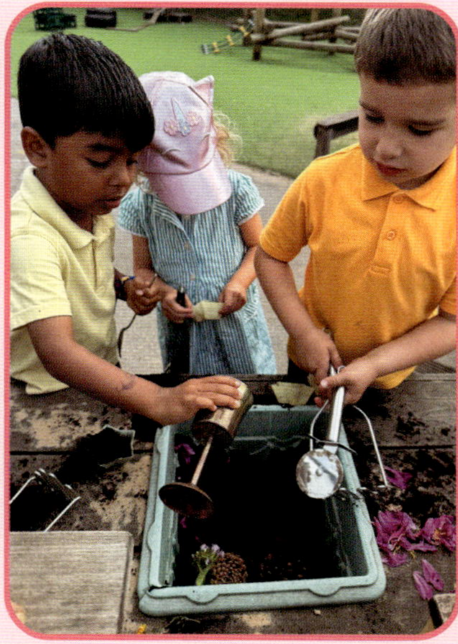

What's in it for the children?

The children can **learn about the start of the growing calendar** and explore new life from plants, spring flowers and growing shoots. They can also develop their **expressive art and design** skills by using nature's colours in their mud kitchen creations.

Taking it forward

- To extend the theme of spring, create an area in the outdoors to teach about growing and looking after flowers and plants.

- Talk about how different plants grow and what they need such as earth, water and sun.

- Discuss the best time of the year to plant bulbs and flowers.

Top tip 

To create spring coloured water for play, add a couple of drops of food colouring. To give it a cloudy appearance, include a splash of milk or a spoonful of cornflour.

Petal omelettes

A tasty breakfast snack

What you need:

- Mud
- Water
- Bowl
- Scoops or spoons
- Frying pan
- Nature finds such as petals
- Spatula

What's in it for the children?

The children develop their **hand strength** and **fine motor skills** through pulling and tearing the petals. Choosing how to decorate the omelettes with the petals and different items from nature helps the children to develop their **expressive art and design skills**.

Taking it forward

- Create instructions about how to make petal omelettes to inspire friends to make them in the mud kitchen. Turn it into a recipe book!

What to do:

1. Mix the mud and water in a bowl to create a 'muddy egg' mixture.

2. Show the children how to scoop the muddy egg mixture into a frying pan.

3. Encourage the children to tear the items from nature or petals and add them into the frying pan.

4. On the mud kitchen hob, show the children how to 'fry' the omelette for a few minutes.

5. Help the children to use the spatula to turn the petal omelette over.

6. Encourage the children to decorate the omelettes with a few more petals on top to garnish and 'serve'.

Top tip 

Grow flowers or ask for used and expired bunches from others so that you can use the petals in the mud kitchen.

Easter mud kitchen

An Easter extravaganza

What you need:

- Easter decorations
- Bowls
- Mud
- Egg boxes
- Items from nature
- Jugs or jars
- Pots and pans

What's in it for the children?

This type of play allows children to **explore festivals and traditions** and make sense of the world around them, whilst also fostering **imaginative play**.

Taking it forward

- Eggs represent new life and rebirth: link egg play in the mud kitchen to learning about the life cycle of chickens.

- Explore further egg play to help children understand links to Easter and why it is celebrated.

Health & Safety

Ensure that egg boxes are clean before use.

What to do:

1. Talk to the children about what they know about Easter and why and how it is celebrated.

2. Decorate the mud kitchen with any Easter decorations you may have. Ask friends and family to donate any they no longer use or make your own.

3. Fill the bowls with plenty of mud and include recycled egg boxes.

4. Display natural items in jugs or jars for the children to use.

5. Encourage the children to create Easter inspired recipes such as muddy eggs in the egg boxes or food for the Easter bunny using natural objects in the pots and pans.

6. Once the children have made the food, they could role play leaving it out for the Easter bunny to eat or invite others to 'taste' their creations.

Top tip 

Save packaging from Easter eggs to use in the mud kitchen play after celebrating.

Blossom mud kitchen

Bringing spring to life

What you need:

- Bowls
- Coloured water
- Blossom petals
- Mud
- Utensils
- Measuring jugs (optional)

Health & Safety

Check for allergies of trees and make sure the children wash their hands after use.

What's in it for the children?

The children develop their **language and communication skills** while talking about their blossom creations as well as their **mathematical understanding of capacity** when taking part in basic measuring.

Taking it forward

- Talk to the children about the life cycle of blossom trees and how they grow over the changing seasons.
- Show the children pictures of cherry trees – there are over three hundred different varieties!

What to do:

1. Fill some of the bowls with coloured water (using a splash of food colouring and milk or cornflour) and some of the bowls with mud.

2. Mix the blossom petals into the coloured water. Place a sprinkling of petals in jars, bowls or jugs to use in the blossom play.

3. Encourage the children to use tins and mix, stir and sprinkle the blossoms into the water and mud. Encourage older children to use measuring jugs to develop early understanding of capacity.

4. Encourage the children to make petal puddings, blossom pies, cupcakes and soups and to come up with their own beautiful blossom creations.

Top tip 

When blossom starts to fall from the trees (usually around early April time), take the children on an outing to collect the fallen petals.

Sensory herb mud kitchen
Joy for the senses

What you need:

- A selection of herbs: mint, thyme, lavender, coriander, basil, parsley and rosemary
- Mud
- Safety scissors
- Utensils
- Bowls
- Pots and pans

What's in it for the children?

Using scissors is a great way to help the children to develop their **fine motor skills**. Smelling the variety of herbs and talking about them as they mix, snip and stir provides the children with new sensory experiences and helps to develop their **communication and language skills**.

Taking it forward

- Growing herbs is easy and they do not take up much space. They can be planted in small pots, tubs or planters. Make signs for a herb garden to help identify them.

What to do:

1. Collect a range of herbs and make them available in the mud kitchen.

2. Provide the children with safety scissors alongside mud, utensils, bowls, pots and pans.

3. Encourage the children to use the scissors to snip the herbs and include them in their mud kitchen recipes.

4. Suggest that the children mix the mud and herbs together to create muddy meals and desserts.

5. Talk to the children while they are making their muddy creations. What can they feel when they touch the herbs? What can they smell? What herbs do they like the smell and texture of the most?

Top tip 

Local supermarkets sell small fresh tubs of herbs in pots for a small cost. Pick up a few when shopping to use in mud kitchen play and to plant afterwards.

Health & Safety

Take care with scissors when cutting the herbs and be mindful of children who may be sensitive towards very strong smells.

Herby muffins
A sensory recipe

What you need:

- Water
- Mud
- Bowls
- Spoons
- Muffin tins
- A selection of herbs (see 'sensory herb kitchen' page 35)
- Safety scissors

What's in it for the children?

This is a great sensory experience which also helps to develop the children's **fine motor skills** through using scissors, **communication and language skills** through talking about what they can feel and smell and **expressive art and design skills** through choosing how to decorate their muffins.

Taking it forward

- Play a sensory herb game to identify each herb by smell. Blindfold the children and ask them to smell the herbs individually. Can they name the herb by the scent?

What to do:

1. Make the muffin batter by adding a little water to mud in a large bowl. Stir well.

2. Show the children how to scoop a spoonful of muddy batter into each hole of the muffin tin.

3. Help the children to cut small portions of herbs with safety scissors or pull a few sprigs off with fingers.

4. Ask the children to place the herbs on top of each muffin, encouraging them to choose their own ways to decorate them.

5. Help the children put the filled muffin tray into the mud kitchen oven to 'bake', remove and serve. Encourage the children to take pride in their creations by sharing with others what they have made.

6. Talk to the children about their muffins: which herbs did they use and what did they smell like?

Health & Safety

Always identify each herb carefully before use to ensure it is not confused with a harmful or toxic plant.

Top tip 

Wash the herbs and use them in other sensory play such as water play for a new sensory experience.

Grassy tea

Refreshment using grass and water

What you need:

- A tea set or mugs
- Jugs or a teapot
- Water
- Grass
- Items from nature
- Teaspoons

What's in it for the children?

This activity helps the children to build on **problem solving and collaboration skills** as the children work together to pour the water into each cup to fill it. It will also encourage **social skills** as they take turns pouring and role play serving each other drinks.

Taking it forward

- Set up an outdoor café to include a variety of drinks using items from nature, mud, water and ice (see 'Muddy drinks kitchen', page 16).

- Introduce tea bags, herbs and other items to extend the sensory experience.

Health & Safety

Encourage pretend drinking of the tea and explain that it is not really for drinking.

What to do:

1. Collect mugs, a tea set, jugs and a teapot to use in the play. If using bone china, assess the risk and the age of the children or look for a durable metal set.

2. Fill the jugs and teapot with water.

3. Offer grass and items found in nature for mixing into the tea.

4. Help the children to take turns pouring cups of tea from the teapot and jugs, adding in a sprinkle of grass and items from nature. Stir with teaspoons.

5. Encourage the children to role play serving the cups of tea to their friends.

Top tip ⭐

During the colder months, add warm water to the play to keep little fingers from becoming frozen. Have a discussion about how real cups of tea or coffee can be hot and a potential burning hazard.

Mud kitchen food

Turn pebbles into delicious creations

What you need:

- Smooth pebbles (medium sized)
- Paint
- Paintbrushes
- Varnish

What to do:

1. Gather medium sized smooth pebbles, an assortment of paint colours and a paintbrush.

2. Paint each pebble to resemble an item of food. Easy ones to create are oranges, strawberries, kiwi, fried egg, watermelon, grapes and tomatoes.

3. Once the paint is dry, seal with varnish.

4. Use the painted pebbles as part of creative mud kitchen recipe play and role play.

5. Let the children have a go at painting their own pebbles to play with in the mud kitchen: what kind of food will they paint?

Top tip 

Instead of varnish, the children can use PVA glue as an alternative. This won't last as long but will seal them for a little while when using in mud kitchen play. Chalk pens are a great alternative to paint and work just as well on pebbles.

What's in it for the children?

Painting pebbles is therapeutic and a fun, creative process, which develops the children's **expressive art and design skills** and gives them a sense of **achievement and involvement** as they create items which they can then use in their mud kitchen.

Taking it forward

- Decorate other items from nature such as such as log slices, bark, sticks or leaves to enhance the mud kitchen play.

Health & Safety
Always check the paint and varnish used is child-friendly.

Summer mud kitchen

Muddy fun in the sun

What you need:

- Water
- Ice cube trays or small pots
- Items from nature
- Summer flowers such as sunflowers
- Petals
- Utensils
- Bowls, pots and pans

What's in it for the children?

Providing the children with opportunities for open-ended play helps to foster their **imaginative and creative thinking**. Encouraging the children to explore different textures such as sand, water and ice provides them with a sensory experience and learning about seasonal changes helps to develop their **understanding of the world**.

Taking it forward

- Learn about the different varieties of flowers used, for example sunflowers: grow them from seeds in early March and measure how tall they become.

- Look at the lifecycle of a sunflower from seed to flower. Collect the seeds from the head once grown and save for planting the following year.

What to do:

1. Talk to the children about what they know about summer and what changes in the weather they might expect to see.

2. Ahead of playing in the summer mud kitchen, freeze some of the items from nature in ice cube trays or pots overnight. Once frozen, remove and place into the mud kitchen bowls.

3. Fill the bowls or tubs with mud and add some water for sensory fun.

4. Include plenty of utensils, bowls, pots and pans and tins to enable the children to explore the mud kitchen independently and have an open-ended space to play.

5. Encourage the children to create summer recipes using the nature ice cubes, mud pies, nature cakes, baking ideas and drinks in the sunshine and to talk about what they are making together.

Health & Safety

Always check the variety of flowers used to ensure they are a non-toxic or a non-poisonous type.

Top tip 

Let the children play with items from nature that have been frozen in blocks of ice to keep them cool in hot weather.

Mud burgers
Grill a muddy feast

What's in it for the children?

This activity is great for sensory stimulation and **messy, hands-on play**. Encouraging children to make their own choices about which ingredients to put in their burgers helps to develop their **problem-solving skills** while imaginative barbeque role play helps to develop their **social and communication skills**.

Taking it forward

- Make fries to go with the burger using sticks and twigs.
- Create packaging from recycled card to place the mud burger and fries into.

Health & Safety
Watch out for splinters in the wooden log slices when handling.

What to do:

1. Talk to the children about what might usually go into a burger and how to replicate one with mud.

2. Mix up the mud with a small amount of water in the bowls to create a thick consistency.

3. Show the children how to spread the mud onto the first log slice, which will be used as the burger bun.

4. Encourage the children to add ingredients such as yellow petals for cheese slices, leaves for lettuce, and red petals for tomato slices.

5. Help the children to place the top log slice onto the muddy burger, adding an extra layer to make it into a double burger.

6. Encourage the children to enjoy pretending to eat the burger and have a pretend barbeque!

Top tip ⭐

Try not to add too much mud onto the log slice or it will fall out of the sides.

Leaf and petal kebabs

What you need:

- Sticks
- Potato peelers or child-friendly whittling knives
- An assortment of items from nature such as leaves and petals

What's in it for the children?

Learning how to use tools safely helps the children to take **calculated risks**. Children also develop their **fine and gross motor skills** when using the tools, picking up items from nature and threading them onto the stick.

Taking it forward

- Create a simple pattern when threading the items from nature on the sticks and continue it. Such as leaf, flower, leaf, flower, leaf, flower. Try using a pattern with three items to follow and continue after this.

Health & Safety

When using the peeler or whittling knife, use a glove on the opposite hand to protect skin. Supervise children 1:1 when using tools. Add this to your risk assessment.

What to do:

1. Talk to the children about safety when working with tools such as potato peelers or whittling knives.

2. Encourage the children to choose a stick that is sturdy but not too thick.

3. Show the children how to hold the stick with one hand and the potato peeler or whittling stick in the opposite hand and scrape away at the end of the stick to create a point.

4. Encourage the children to thread the items from nature onto the stick using the pointed end to create a kebab. Talk to them about the items they chose.

5. See if the children can role play grilling on the barbeque mud kitchen.

Top tip 

If choosing not to use a whittling knife or peeler, choose thin sticks that are easy to push through the leaves or a wooden skewer.

Sticky muddy hot dogs
Turn sticks into sausages

What you need:

- Leaves (large and long)
- Mud
- Sticks
- Red or yellow petals

Top tip 

Choose a chunky stick that resembles a sausage shape for the hot dog.

What to do:

1. Help the children to search for a nice big leaf and choose one that is long in shape.
2. Show the children how to spread a layer of mud on the leaf for the stick to sit on.
3. Place the stick into the mud: this is the hot dog sausage.
4. Encourage the children to sprinkle petals onto their hot dogs: red for tomato sauce or yellow for mustard.
5. Gently roll the sides of the leaf upwards and pretend to enjoy eating the sticky, muddy hot dog.

What's in it for the children?

Using the hot dogs during imaginative play helps to develop their **social and communication skills**.

Taking it forward

- Create a hot dog stand so that the children can 'sell' sticky muddy hot dogs to their friends. Take payment in stones and create a menu of options.

Health & Safety

Always check the species of leaves and if taking from low ground it is best to give the leaf a little wash with water before allowing young children to handle.

Muddy ice cream

A favourite treat made from mud

What you need:

- Mud
- Ice cream bowls or recycled ice cream packaging
- Spoons
- Ice cream scoops
- Squirty foam
- Items from nature

What's in it for the children?

This activity helps children to have a sensory experience while feeling and touching the mud, experiencing different textures whilst also boosting their confidence to **'have a go'** and **try something new**.

Taking it forward

- Create a muddy ice cream menu including plenty of different flavours.
- Make ice cream cones from leaves or folded card.

What to do:

1. Talk to the children about what ice cream flavours and toppings they like the most.

2. Mix the mud and fill the recycled ice cream tub with it. Include an ice cream scoop.

3. Use the mud as chocolate ice cream. Show the children how to scoop out and fill the ice cream bowls with one or two scoops.

4. Discuss with the children what toppings they might use: a stick for a flake and dried flower sprinkles.

5. Include squirty foam to create a different flavour and drizzle watery mud on top for chocolate sauce, or swap mud for wet sand to create caramel ice cream.

Top tip 

Ask family and friends to save their washed ice cream tubs and packaging for use in the ice cream mud kitchen.

Beach themed mud kitchen

Bring the seaside to the mud kitchen

What you need:

- Sand
- Bowls
- Water
- Blue food colouring
- Shells
- Pebbles
- Recycled beach themed décor
- Scoops, buckets and spades
- Toy sea creatures (optional)

What to do:

1. Talk to the children about what they already know about the beach; show them pictures and read them stories about the seaside.

2. Swap the mud in the mud kitchen bowls for sand and provide blue coloured water (made by mixing water with a few drops of blue food colouring) to replicate the ocean.

3. Include bunting or other recycled beach décor in the mud kitchen for a fun, seaside feel.

4. Use buckets, spades, shells, pebbles, artificial seaweed or sea creatures to create the beach theme.

5. Encourage the children to explore what happens when the water and sand are mixed together. Help them to create rock pools, sandcastles or explore the materials.

6. Encourage the children to make seaside themed recipes such as ice creams, fish and chips and picnic food using the sand and items.

✚ Health & Safety

Keep the sand bowls covered when not in use to stop insects or small animals using them.

Top tip 

It is illegal to take shells and pebbles from UK beaches; buy them online or from seaside or craft shops instead.

What's in it for the children?

If children have already experienced a trip to the beach, this is a great way to **consolidate their learning** and allow them to **express themselves through play**. Some children may not have had this prior experience; exploring the items and feeling the sand between their fingers will give them a new joyful sensory experience.

Taking it forward

- Continue the beach theme setup elsewhere such as sandpits, small world play, messy areas and water areas.
- Learn about water safety at the beach.

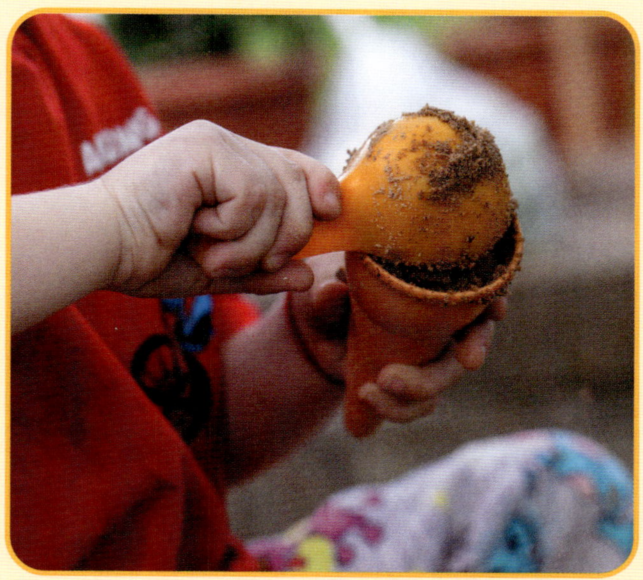

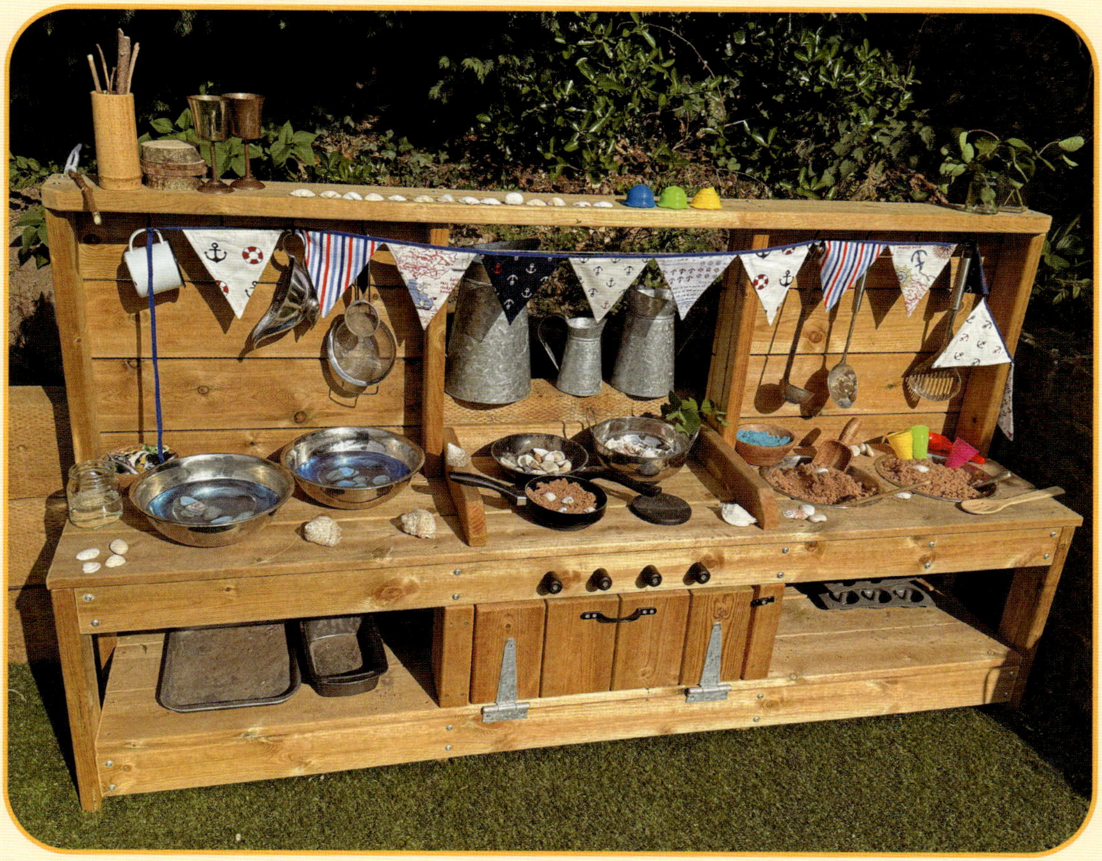

Citrus mud kitchen

A feast for the senses

What you need:

- Bowls
- Mud
- Water
- Citrus fruit: lemons, limes and oranges
- Utensils
- Jugs
- Pans
- Graters
- Tongs

What's in it for the children?

This is a fabulous form of sensory play as the citrus fruit heightens the children's sense of smell, touch and sight when using them. The activity also helps the children learn **new vocabulary** and develop their **communication and language skills**.

Taking it forward

- A tasting citrus fruits session can add an extra sensory element of taste.
- Bake or create (non-muddy) edible recipes with citrus fruits.
- Research how to grow citrus fruits and try this out in your setting.

Top tip 

Be mindful of children's sensitivities to smell. Citrus fruit smells can be overwhelming and this may not be pleasant to all children.

What to do:

1. Talk to the children about what they already know about citrus fruit and introduce new vocabulary such as rind, skin, lemon, lime, orange and grapefruit.

2. Fill the bowls with mud and water.

3. Enhance the mud kitchen with bowls, utensils, jugs, pans, graters and tongs.

4. Slice some of the citrus fruits prior to play and leave some whole. Place them into the mud kitchen.

5. Allow the children to investigate the citrus fruits and incorporate into their mud kitchen play.

6. Encourage the children to create citrus mud pies, citrus soups, citrus drinks and any other recipes they can think of.

7. Use the grater against the citrus rind as a garnish on the recipes or pick up the slices with tongs to include in the mud kitchen baking.

8. Link this activity to music learning by singing the nursery rhyme 'Oranges and Lemons'.

Health & Safety

- Check for allergies.
- Wash citrus fruits before use to eliminate any contact with pesticide residue.

Water and ice kitchen

Explore the elements

What you need:

- Water
- Food colouring (optional)
- Items from nature
- Ice trays
- Containers
- Child-friendly hammers
- Scoops

What's in it for the children?

The children will gain an early **understanding of science** and the properties of liquids and solids. By experimenting with melting and watching as the ice turns into water, the children will gain first hand experiences of a scientific process.

Taking it forward

- The children can find out what makes the ice melt quicker, such as warm water or leaving in the sun.

- In the colder months, explore leaving water outdoors overnight in containers to find out what happens.

What to do:

1. In advance, fill containers with found items from nature and pour water over (leaving a little space at the top). Freeze overnight. Remove the frozen ice blocks from the containers and place into the mud kitchen.

2. Fill the bowls with water and add drops of food colouring if wanting to achieve different colours.

3. Provide ice cubes, small hammers, scoops and containers.

4. Encourage the children to explore the ice and water. The children can scoop, mix and stir together or find out how to excavate the nature items from the ice.

5. Help the children to use the hammers to break the ice and find out what happens over the day to each piece of ice.

6. Talk to the children while they are exploring: what can they see happening to the ice the longer it stays out in the sun? Why do they think this is happening?

Top tip 

Children can wear gloves when handling ice to protect fingers and delicate skin. Waterproof gloves work best in this type of play.

Health & Safety

Don't use salt on the ice as this can cause a reaction on the skin if touched.

Nature milkshakes

Therapeutic and fun!

What you need:

- Plastic cups, milkshake cups or bottles
- Water
- Items from nature
- Mud
- Milk or cornflour (optional)
- Safety scissors
- Jugs or a water dispenser
- Sticks

What's in it for the children?

Playing with water and natural elements can help with **mindfulness** and be therapeutic to children. Using measuring jugs helps to develop the children's **mathematical understanding of capacity** and using scissors helps to build **hand strength** and develop the children's **fine motor skills**.

Taking it forward

- Include ice, crushed ice, more mud or sand to give the milkshakes a different texture.

What to do:

1. Provide a selection of jugs, plastic cups or milkshake cups and bottles to create the nature milkshakes in. Place the items from nature in pots.

2. Fill up the water dispenser or use jugs with water in. Include a small amount of milk or cornflour to turn the water a cloudy colour. Encourage older children to use measuring jugs to develop their mathematical understanding of capacity and measurement.

3. Encourage the children to use safety scissors to snip a few leaves or items from nature into small pieces.

4. Encourage the children to pour the cloudy milkshake mixture into the cups and add a small spoonful of dry mud.

5. Encourage the children to stir the mixture with a stick and sprinkle the chopped items from nature for decoration.

Top tip 

If providing jugs for pouring, ensure they are only half full and an appropriate size for young children.

Wedding mud cake

Love in every layer

What you need:

- Cups
- Piping bags
- Mud
- Log slices
- Nature decorations

 **Health & Safety**

If making a large cake with many log slices it will become heavy. Be mindful of the cake toppling over onto young children.

What's in it for the children?

Working together to **stack and balance** the logs teaches **gross motor skills** and **coordination** as well as **co-operation and teamwork**, while putting the logs into size order helps to develop **mathematical thinking**. Squeezing the piping bag is great **fine motor skills** work for growing fingers.

Taking it forward

- Set up a whole wedding party (or change the theme to a birthday party).
- Create invitations using pressed flowers and bunting decorations by hammering items from nature onto material.

What to do:

1. Talk to the children about different types of celebrations, such as birthdays and weddings, and when they might have special types of cake.

2. Fill a piping bag with mud. Placing the bag in a cup and folding over the edges is the easiest way to keep it sturdy when filling with mud.

3. Ask the children to work together to put the log slices in order from largest to smallest. Use the largest for the bottom of the cake and the smallest at the top.

4. Ask the children to work together to spread a layer of mud onto the largest log slice and stack the next log slice on top. Repeat until the log slices are piled up and sandwiched together with mud.

5. Show the children how to use the piping bag filled with mud to pipe decorations around the edges of the cake and on the top log slice.

6. Encourage the children to embellish the cake with found items from nature by pressing them into the piped mud.

Top tip ⭐

When filling the piping bag with mud, make sure the mud is quite sloppy (but not too watery). This will help it flow out of the bag smoothly. Choose a thick bag as a thin one will split with the mud inside.

Muddy cupcakes

A delicious muddy treat

What you need:

- Bowls
- Mud
- Water (a small amount)
- Spoons
- Silicone cupcake cases
- Petals or nature finds
- Coloured chalk
- Small graters

What's in it for the children?

Mixing, grating and scooping are great for developing **fine motor skills** and **hand eye coordination**. When playing with others, children will negotiate and cooperate, learning to **take turns** when making their creations.

Taking it forward

- Try using a piping bag containing mud to pipe swirls onto the muddy cupcakes.

- Swap the mud for sand and create some sandy cupcakes. Shells would make excellent toppings for them.

What to do:

1. Mix up some muddy cupcake mixture in a bowl, add a little water if needed to make a batter like consistency.

2. Ask the children to use a spoon to scoop mud into the silicone cupcake cases.

3. Encourage the children to add natural toppings such as petals, flowers, small pinecones or stones.

4. Help the children to use the chalk and a small grater to grate coloured sprinkles onto the cupcakes.

Top tip 

Leave the muddy cupcakes out in the sun or inside the mud kitchen oven for a few days. The mud will harden and they will be ready to pretend to eat.

Health & Safety

When using the small grater, encourage the children to move the chalk slowly and carefully so that the grater does not scrape the skin on their fingers.

Muddy log pizzas
Italian pizza chefs in the outdoors

What you need:

- Log slices
- Mud
- Spoons or spatulas
- Yellow chalk
- Graters (small)
- Items from nature

What's in it for the children?

Creating new muddy, outdoor inspired recipes and turning mud and logs into something so familiar, yet such fun, will boost **creativity** and allows the children to use their **imaginations**. By building on previous experiences and acting them out in play, the children can begin to **make sense of the world around them**.

Taking it forward

- Pizza restaurant role play: the children can create their own menus for the different flavoured pizza creations they come up with and take orders from their friends.

- Create an outdoor pretend pizza oven by using bricks and planks of wood.

Health & Safety

Watch out for splinters in the wooden log slices and supervise children carefully when grating chalk.

What to do:

1. Talk to the children about different food from around the world and explain that pizza comes from Italy. Discuss with the children about the different toppings they like to have on pizza.

2. Encourage the children to work in groups or pairs and choose a log slice for the pizza base.

3. Ask the children to work together using a spoon or spatula to spread mud over the top of the log slice pizza base to cover it. This will be the tomato sauce!

4. Grate yellow chalk onto the mud base for cheese.

5. Encourage the children to choose different items from nature for the toppings. For example, a ham and pineapple (Hawaiian) could be made from yellow leaves for the pineapple and pink petals for the ham.

6. Ask the children to 'bake' the muddy pizzas in the mud kitchen oven and then serve. They could try using a toy pizza cutter to pretend slicing the muddy pizzas up.

Top tip ⭐

Mix a little water into the mud to ensure it can spread easily onto the log slices. Make sure it's not too runny as it won't spread.

Chocolate 'muddy' cheesecake

Gourmet muddy treats

What you need:

- Jars or pots (small)
- Mud
- Water
- Wet sand
- Spoons
- Small leaves

What to do:

1. Choose a jar or pot suitable for a muddy cheesecake. A round one is a great option.

2. Show the children how to use a layer of wet sand in the bottom of the pot for the 'biscuit' base. Ask them to press down with a spoon.

3. Ask the children to scoop a spoonful of mud into the pot (on top of the sand) for the cheesecake, pressing down gently with the spoon.

4. Encourage the children to decorate the top layer with small leaves for the topping. A little drizzle of muddy water on top for the sauce or a sprinkle of sand will finish the muddy cheesecake off.

5. Leave to 'chill' in the mud kitchen and serve once cool.

What's in it for the children?

The children develop their **mathematical vocabulary** when discussing concepts such as 'full' and 'empty' when filling the jars or pots. This activity will give an early introduction into capacity as the children fill each jar with muddy ingredients.

Taking it forward

- Explore capacity in varying sizes of containers using mud, water or sand.

 **Health & Safety**

If choosing a glass jar, try to use these in a place where they will not get broken and smashed or choose a more durable option if children are likely to drop them.

Top tip 

Save dessert jars from cheesecakes or pudding pots and recycle them into muddy cheesecake jars.

Nature biscuits

Bake a tasty treat in the mud kitchen

What you need:

- Log slices
- Baking trays
- Mud
- Spoons or spatulas
- Items from nature

✚ Health & Safety

Always check the species of petals and leaves, to ensure no poisonous varieties are used. Wash hands after handling.

What to do:

1. Show the children how to use the log slices as biscuits by laying them out onto a baking tray.

2. Help the children to spread muddy 'chocolate' topping onto the log slice biscuits by using a spoon or spatula.

3. Encourage the children to be creative when adding the toppings such as dried crushed petals, leaves or grass on top of the mud.

4. Ask the children to 'bake' their biscuits in the mud kitchen and role play serving with a cup of grassy tea! (See page 37).

What's in it for the children?

This activity helps the children to learn **early mathematical concepts** such as **sharing** the ingredients out between the biscuits, **counting** how many biscuits the children 'baked' in the mud kitchen and **identifying shapes**. Imaginative role play helps to develop their **social and communication skills**.

Taking it forward

- Try different ways of making cookies. For example, thick mud used with cookie cutters or on different kinds of bases such as flat rocks, bark pieces or cardboard.

Top tip 

Ask friends or relatives for their bunches of wilted flowers that are destined for the recycling, especially around celebrations such as Valentine's Day or Mother's Day.

Dirt and stick brownies

A muddy treat with extra crunch

What you need:

- Mud
- Water (a small amount)
- Square tins
- Spoons
- Sticks

Health & Safety
Wash hands after handling sticks foraged from the outdoors.

What's in it for the children?

Dividing the brownies into equal portions helps to build early **mathematical concepts**, such as understanding **shape, space and measure** in a practical way. Choosing how to decorate the brownies using sticks or twigs helps to develop the children's **expressive art and design skills**.

Taking it forward

- Bake real chocolate brownies in the oven and compare to the process of making dirt stick brownies. Which ones look the tastiest? Mud or chocolate?

What to do:

1. Stir a splash of water into some mud to make a thick muddy mixture for the brownies.

2. Show the children how to spread the mixture into a square tin and smooth down using the back of a spoon.

3. Ask the children to work together to score the brownies gently with a stick to make nine equal square parts.

4. Suggest that the children top each square with thin sticks or twigs and choose how they want to decorate each square.

5. Encourage the children to 'bake' their brownies in the mud kitchen and serve with muddy ice cream (see page 43).

Top tip 

Collect sticks when out walking to use in the mud kitchen at a later date. Choose a variety of sizes.

Nature jam scones

Jam or cream first?

What you need:

- Log slices
- Squirty foam
- Water
- Petals
- Pestle and mortar or stick and bowl

Health & Safety
Check for allergies or skin sensitivities to foam.

What's in it for the children?

This activity is great for the children's **imagination and creativity**. They can imagine themselves as a baker or a chef, creating exciting recipes. When working together, they can discuss the ingredients and how to make the scones, developing their **social skills**.

Taking it forward

- Bake pretend scones using salt dough as this will harden and is a great alternative to the log slices. Use a mixture of 1 cup of flour, ½ cup of water and ½ cup of salt. Add pebbles for a fruit scone.

What to do:

1. Show the children how to use two log slices as the scone halves.
2. Encourage the children to squirt some foam onto the log slice to become the 'cream'.
3. Show the children how to crush the petals and mix with a little water. Use a pestle and mortar or a bowl and thick stick.
4. Encourage the children to spread a layer of petal jam onto the cream.
5. If the children prefer jam before cream, complete step 4 first.
6. Sandwich the two halves together and serve as part of a muddy afternoon tea (see page 59).

Top tip 

A squirt of washing up liquid in a bowl of water whisked with a mixer creates a foamy mixture that can be used instead of squirty foam from a can.

Takeaway nature rice

What you need:

- Takeaway tubs
- Dry mud
- Spoons
- Stones and pebbles
- Frying pans or woks

Top tip 

After a takeaway, save and wash the packaging it arrived in to use in play. Alternatively, pick some up cheaply online or in home shops.

What's in it for the children?

Role play scenarios are key in child development as they make sense of the world around them. It helps to evoke **creativity** and inspires them to use their **imagination** when playing. Role playing in a takeaway or shop scenario helps children to gain an early **mathematical understanding of money**.

Taking it forward

- Create an outdoor delivery car or motorbike using large loose parts such as planks, logs, tyres and crates to deliver the nature takeaway rice to customers.

What to do:

1. Collect takeaway tubs and wash them before use.

2. Show the children how to crumble the dry mud into the frying pan and mix in small pebbles as the rice.

3. Show the children how to 'fry' the pretend vegetables (leaves and other items from nature) into the pan and stir them all together.

4. Encourage the children to scoop the nature rice into the takeaway dishes and place a lid on to 'keep warm'.

5. Encourage the children to role play having their own takeaways and delivering the nature rice to the customers. What else could they serve in their takeaway and how much would it cost?

Health & Safety

Small pebbles can cause a choking hazard. Use larger pebbles if young children place items in their mouth or replace with an alternative such as chopped up sticks.

Muddy sandwiches

Mud and leaves make a delicious sandwich

What you need:

- Mud
- Water
- Bowls
- Spoons
- Leaves
- Items from nature (for the filling)

⊕ **Health & Safety**
Always check the species of leaves and items from nature that you are using for any poisonous varieties.

What's in it for the children?

Stirring and spreading the mud mixture and lifting the log slices helps to develop children's **gross motor skills**, while plucking petals helps to develop the children's **fine motor skills**. Teamwork and sharing helps to build on the children's **social and communication skills**.

Taking it forward

- Create new fillings for the sandwiches such as 'tuna muddyaise' or ham made from petals.

What to do:

1. Ask the children what their favourite sandwich fillings are and explain that they will be making sandwiches in the mud kitchen.

2. Show the children how to mix up some muddy filling by stirring mud and water in a bowl.

3. Encourage the children to find two large leaves to use as the bread.

4. Show the children how to lay a leaf down and fill with the muddy mixture.

5. Ask the children to add some extra ingredients such as dandelion petals for grated cheese and red petals as tomatoes.

6. Encourage the children to role play serving the tasty mud sandwich on a log plate with a side salad of grass and leaves, and sharing together.

Top tip 

When mixing up the mud filling, don't add too much water or it will become quite runny.

Muddy doughnuts

Turn mud into the round, fried, dough favourite

What you need:

- Mud
- Water
- Items from nature
- Doughnut pan or mould (optional)

What's in it for the children?

This activity helps the children to use their **imagination** and **expressive art and design skills** when decorating their doughnuts. Rolling mud into a ball helps to develop **hand strength** and **fine motor skills**.

Taking it forward

- Ask the children to create a menu of different flavoured muddy doughnuts: what's the most interesting doughnut flavour they can think of?
- Link the activity to learning about shapes. Could the children make a square or triangular doughnut?

What to do:

1. Mix up a muddy mixture that is nice and thick.

2. Show the children how to use a doughnut mould or pan to fill the space with mud to create muddy doughnuts.

3. Alternatively, show the children how to use their hands to create a ball shape out of mud and push their finger through the middle to make the doughnut hole.

4. Encourage the children to 'bake' their doughnuts in the mud kitchen oven. Leaving for a few days in warm weather will turn the mud hard.

5. Allow the children to decorate their doughnuts with toppings such as petals, tiny leaves or flowers to create different flavours.

Top tip ⭐

Silicone doughnut moulds are a great addition to the mud kitchen as they're flexible and can be easily washed. Use on a flat surface when making muddy doughnuts.

Afternoon tea mud kitchen

A twist on the British tradition

What you need:

- Mud
- Water
- Jugs or a water dispenser
- Spoons
- Items from nature
- Tea sets
- Teapots
- Cake stands
- Cupcake cases

Top tip 

Ask relatives and friends to donate unwanted cake stands or tea sets they no longer use.

What's in it for the children?

This imaginative and fun activity is great for developing the children's **social, language and communication skills**. Role playing making afternoon tea and sharing it with their friends instils a **sense of pride** in their work and working together encourages **teamwork and sharing**.

Taking it forward

- Create decorations such as bunting using white material cut into triangles.
- Use a technique called 'Hapa Zome' which means the Japanese art of hammering nature pigments onto material. Lay the flowers or petals onto the material and hit with a hammer. Hang up in the mud kitchen to decorate.

What to do:

1. Set up a range of items for the afternoon tea such as a tea set, mugs, a teapot, jugs, a cake stand and utensils.

2. Show the children how to create some recipes such as grassy tea (page 37), muddy cupcakes (page 50) muddy sandwiches (page 57) or nature jam scones (page 55) and include them in the afternoon tea mud kitchen.

3. Help the children to present the muddy creations on the cake stand, plates or a large log slice.

4. Show the children how to pour cups of grassy tea or hot chocolate and serve them to their friends.

5. Help the children dish up some of the delicious muddy sandwiches and follow with a tasty mud cake and muddy cup of tea.

Health & Safety

Use cold water only in the tea pot, jugs or dispensers rather than hot water to prevent children from burning their skin.

Phonics mud kitchen

'M' is for mud!

What you need:

- Mud
- Water
- Paintbrushes
- Baking trays
- Sounds and letters on logs or nature letters

What to do:

1. Fill bowls with mud and jugs with water.

2. Provide paintbrushes, trays and utensils.

3. Display sounds and letters made from items from nature or written on log slices.

4. Mix muddy paint using the mud and water in bowls.

5. Show the children how to dip the paintbrushes into the muddy paint and use to recreate the phonics sounds displayed around the mud kitchen.

6. Guide and encourage the children to write their names using the muddy paint.

7. Play phonics games such as matching the log or nature letters to initial sounds of items found in the mud kitchen, for example 'm' for mud, 'p' for petals, 'j' for jug.

8. Provide large scale surfaces for children to use the muddy paint on such as blackboards, sheets hung up or large easels beside the mud kitchen. This will enable the children to cross the midline when mark making, which is an essential skill to build on in the Early Years.

What's in it for the children?

The children learn **sounds and letters** and apply their **phonics knowledge** in fun and different ways outside of the classroom. They can consolidate their phonics learning in an outdoor environment, surrounded by the natural world.

Taking it forward

- Make nature paintbrushes for making marks and creating letters and keep them in the mud kitchen to encourage further use. Use a stick, items from nature and a pipe cleaner or string to tie at the end.

 **Top tip**

Meet the children where they are at in their stage of learning. If the children aren't ready to use letters and sounds yet, include pre-writing patterns instead and encourage mark making of wavy lines, swirls and zigzags prior to learning the formation of letters.

Maths mud kitchen

Outdoor learning through play

What you need:

- Weighing scales
- Numbers on logs or nature numbers
- Nature finds for counting
- 5 or 10 frames (age dependent)

What to do:

1. Fill the bowls with mud and include a water source.

2. Include a selection of nature finds that are varying weights and sizes such as pebbles, pinecones, leaves, sticks, acorns, conkers, sycamore seeds etc. There are many different ways to encourage maths learning in the mud kitchen:

   a. When children are playing with their mud creations, inspire the use of weighing items to find out which are the heaviest or to identify how much of each ingredient is needed in the recipe.

   b. Count out toppings onto each recipe and count scoops of mud into the bowls as the children play.

   c. Talk about the containers and use vocabulary such as 'full' or 'empty', identifying how the children know if the container is full.

   d. Lead maths scavenger hunts to promote number recognition: display a number in the mud kitchen and ask the children to find that number of items from nature.

The mud kitchen is the perfect space to **explore all things related to maths**, naturally through play. Children will **weigh** their items, learning about balance and weight. They can **count** items from nature onto their muddy creations or **discuss capacity** when filling the tins and pans with mud or water.

Taking it forward

- Introduce an element of 'measure'. Try making rulers with pieces of wood painted with blackboard paint. Write numbers on. Encourage measurement of sticks and items in the mud kitchen or how long/tall/short the mud creations are. Model measure related vocabulary during play.

Top tip ⭐

Collect nature items from different seasons to enhance the maths mud kitchen. Autumn has many wonderful pieces to use such as sticks, pinecones, large and small leaves, seeds and pebbles. .